FIGHTING FISH

David M. Schwartz is an award-winning author of children's books, on a wide variety of topics, loved by children around the world. Dwight Kuhn's scientific expertise and artful eye work together with the camera to capture the awesome wonder of the natural world.

Please visit our web site at: www.garethstevens.com
For a free color catalog describing Gareth Stevens Publishing's list of high-quality books and multimedia programs, call 1-800-542-2595 (USA) or 1-800-461-9120 (Canada).
Gareth Stevens Publishing's Fax: (414) 332-3567.

Library of Congress Cataloging-in-Publication Data

Schwartz, David M.
    Fighting fish / by David M. Schwartz; photographs by Dwight Kuhn. — North American ed.
      p. cm. — (Life cycles: a springboards into science series)
    Includes bibliographical references and index.
    ISBN 0-8368-2972-7 (lib. bdg.)
    1. Betta—Juvenile literature. [1. Siamese fighting fish.] I. Kuhn, Dwight, ill. II. Title.
  QL638.B347S39 2001
  597'.7—dc21   2001031463

This North American edition first published in 2001 by
Gareth Stevens Publishing
A World Almanac Education Group Company
330 West Olive Street, Suite 100
Milwaukee, WI 53212 USA

First published in the United States in 1999 by Creative Teaching Press, Inc., P.O. Box 2723, Huntington Beach, CA 92647-0723.
Text © 1999 by David M. Schwartz; photographs © 1999 by Dwight Kuhn. Additional end matter © 2001 by Gareth Stevens, Inc.

Gareth Stevens editor: Mary Dykstra

Printed in the United States of America

1 2 3 4 5 6 7 8 9 05 04 03 02 01

FIGHTING FISH

by David M. Schwartz
photographs by Dwight Kuhn

A SPRINGBOARDS INTO

SCIENCE

SERIES

Gareth Stevens Publishing
A WORLD ALMANAC EDUCATION GROUP COMPANY

This colorful fish looks as if it fell into a bucket of red paint! It is a Siamese fighting fish, or betta. Male bettas come in many bright colors. The colors get even brighter when the fish are excited.

Siamese fighting fish really do fight! A male betta attacks any other male that comes too close. If the loser is lucky, he gets away with a few torn fins. Sometimes the two fish keep fighting until one of them is seriously hurt or killed.

Of course, male bettas do more than just fight. Before mating, a male betta builds a floating nest. First, he gulps air and blows tiny bubbles that are coated with sticky saliva.

Then the betta pushes the
bubbles together to make a
raft at the surface of the water.
This bubble raft is the betta's nest.

When a female betta swims by, the male betta curls around her, and she begins to lay hundreds of eggs. The male fertilizes the eggs. Then, before the eggs can sink to the bottom, he collects them in his mouth and blows them into the bubble nest. The bubbles protect the eggs.

In a few days, the eggs hatch into tiny babies called fry. Each fry has a large yolk sac on its belly. The yolk provides food for the fry.

For a day or two, the fry stay in the bubble nest for safety. Then the babies leave. They can take care of themselves right away.

13

When the betta fry are several weeks old, they are much larger, and their yolk sacs have disappeared.

Now they must catch all their food. Betta fry eat tiny animals that are floating in the water.

Male and female betta fry look about the same until they are one year old. Then male and female bettas look very different. Males are larger and more colorful, and their long fins droop like flags. Soon this male betta will build a bubble nest and look for a female mate. Together they will start another generation of bettas.

Can you put these steps in the life cycle of a betta in order?

attacks (v): goes after something or someone in a violent, angry way.

betta: another name for a Siamese fighting fish, which is a type of brightly colored, tropical freshwater fish.

coated: covered with a layer of something.

droop: hang or bend downward.

fertilizes: brings male and female cells together so a new plant or animal can grow.

fins: the thin, flat, fan-shaped parts that stick out from the body of a fish on its back, sides, and tail to help with movement and balance.

generation: all of the young that are born during a particular time period.

hatch: come, or break, out of an egg.

mating: joining male and female cells together to produce young.

raft: a floating platform.

sac: part of an animal that looks like a bag or a pouch full of liquid.

saliva: watery fluid in the mouth.

Siamese: from the country of Thailand, which used to be called Siam.

surface: the outside or boundary, usually at the top of something.

yolk: the part of an egg that contains food for a developing baby animal.

ACTIVITIES

Go Fish for Colors
Like male bettas, many fish are colorful. Visit a pet store and go "fishing" for colors. First, fold a piece of paper into eight sections. In each section, draw a large colored dot with a crayon or marker. Use a different color in each section. Take this paper to the pet store and look for fish that match each color. At home, draw the fish you saw next to the dot of its color.

Small Fry
Baby fish are called "fry." Make a list of other animals and what their babies are called. For example, baby sheep are lambs, and baby cows are calves. If you need help, look at school or in the library for books about baby animals. Make a game by writing the names of adult animals on pieces of cardboard. Then pick a card and say the name for that animal's babies.

Fish Tank Art
Make a colorful fish tank that you will never have to clean! Ask an adult to help you cut the center out of a paper plate so you have a large ring. Tape blue plastic wrap over the opening of the ring. Now draw several colorful fish in the center of a second paper plate. You can draw in some seaweed and shells, too. Staple the plates together to see your fish tank.

The Need for Nests
Male bettas make bubble nests to protect their babies. Other animals make nests, too, or protect their babies in other ways. Look in books or on the Internet to find interesting nests and other ways animals protect their babies. Write down the name of each animal. Next to each name, draw a picture of the nest or the way that animal protects its babies.

More Books to Read

Fish. All About Pets (series). Helen Frost and Gail Saunders-Smith (Pebble Books)

Fish. A First Discovery Book. Gallimard Jeunesse (Scholastic)

Fish. Wonderful World of Animals (series). Beatrice MacLeod (Gareth Stevens)

Learning About Aquarium Fish. Steven James Petruccio (Dover)

What Is a Fish? The Science of Living Things (series). Bobbie Kalman (Crabtree)

What's It Like to Be a Fish? Let's-Read-and-Find-Out Science (series). Wendy Pfeffer (HarperCollins)

Videos

For the Love of Animals: Tropical Fish. (GCG Productions)

What Is a Fish? (Film Ideas)

The World of Fish. (Kimbo Educational)

Web Sites

members.aol.com/andrerich/aquarium/breeding.htm

www.geocities.com/dynarb/

www. prettybirdie.com/betta/betta.htm

Some web sites stay current longer than others. For additional web sites, use a good search engine to locate the following topics: *aquariums, bettas, fighting fish, fish,* and *pets.*

INDEX

air 8

babies 12, 13
bettas 5, 6, 8, 9, 10, 14, 15, 16
bubbles 8, 9, 10, 13, 16

colors 5, 16

eating 15
eggs 10, 12

females 10, 16
fertilizing 10
fighting 6, 8
fins 6, 16
food 12, 15
fry 12, 13, 14, 15, 16

hatching 12

males 5, 6, 8, 10, 16
mates 16
mating 8, 16
mouths 10

nests 8, 9, 10, 13, 16

protecting 10

safety 13
saliva 8
Siamese fighting fish 5, 6
swimming 10

water 9, 15

yolk sacs 12, 14